YOU WERE BORN TO BE A SAINT

Written and Illustrated
by Kortnee Senn

Copyright © Kortnee Senn. All rights reserved.

No part of this book may be reproduced by any means
without the written permission of the author,
except brief portions quoted for purpose of review.

Published by Studio Senn
www.studiosenn.com

Printed in PRC

First Edition 2020

ISBN: 978-1-7354508-0-3

For my children.

May you feel the call to Sainthood

and pursue it with all your heart.

You were born to be a Saint. I can tell. Can you?

With so many to pick from, which one will you choose?

There are thousands of Saints, each one so unique,

with diverse interests and talents.

Let's just take a peek!

A you're a writer like Saint Thomas Aquinas.

Perhaps like Saint Adelaide they'll call you 'Your Highness'

or maybe like Albert your niche will be science.

B you're a healer like beloved Saint Blaise.

Or like Saint Bernadette you'll see Our Lady's sweet gaze

and sharing your story will help others give praise

because you were born to be a Saint!

C you're called to the life of a Carmelite nun.

They've produced many Saints and it could be fun!

They spend their lives serving

'til the race has been won.

D like Saints Damien and Dymphna you'll tend to the sick,

caring for their wellbeing, praying that they heal quick.

When you're helping others things just seem to click

because you were born to be a Saint!

E like Elizabeth, you're drawn to education,
making sure children have a solid foundation.

Teaching them about Christ is a noble vocation.

F you're Saint Francis, letting the Gospel be heard

by every creature, even the birds.

Your heart comes alive when you're preaching the Word

because you were born to be a Saint!

 perhaps like Saints Gregory and Gertrude

they'll call you 'The Great,'

and your influence will have no expiration date.

You can start on this now,

there's no need to wait.

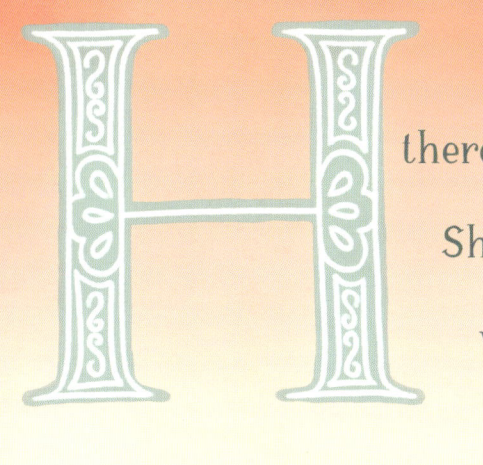

H there's Saint Helen, who unearthed a big mystery.

She found the true cross,

which was quite a huge victory!

Maybe someday like her you'll

preserve our Church history

because you were born to be a Saint!

I you're blessed Isidore,

and

J Josephine.

Saints hail from north to south

and every place in between!

What makes you unique deserves to be seen.

K you could offer up hardships like the Mohawk, Kateri.

Every person has a cross we are each called to carry.

The road to Heaven doesn't have to be scary

because you were born to be a Saint!

L you're Lidwina and

M you're Saint Martin, given a patronage you can put your whole heart in. Interceding for others is where you get started.

you're Saint Nicholas, but I know what you're thinking.

There's more than just one (picture me winking).

You too could help priests and

keep the true Church from shrinking

because you were born to be a Saint!

O there's Our Lady, known under so many titles.
She was Jesus's first and greatest disciple.

Perhaps one day like her you'll start a revival.

P you're a Saintly priest; there are too many to list.

Bringing Christ to the people is a call to assist.

And while the job may be hard, you boldly persist

because you were born to be a Saint!

There are plenty of Saints that start with

Q, R and S

You could be the brave martyr Saint Quirinus,

and like Reparata and Sebastian, give your life for Jesus.

You're tough Mother Teresa, to Calcutta you'll go.

Bringing supplies to the needy, great kindness you'll show.

You'll start a new order that will continue to grow

because you were born to be a Saint!

U you'll become a legend like Saint Ursula and her friends.

They stood up for themselves

and for Christ 'til the end.

Stick with your companions

who share your faith to defend.

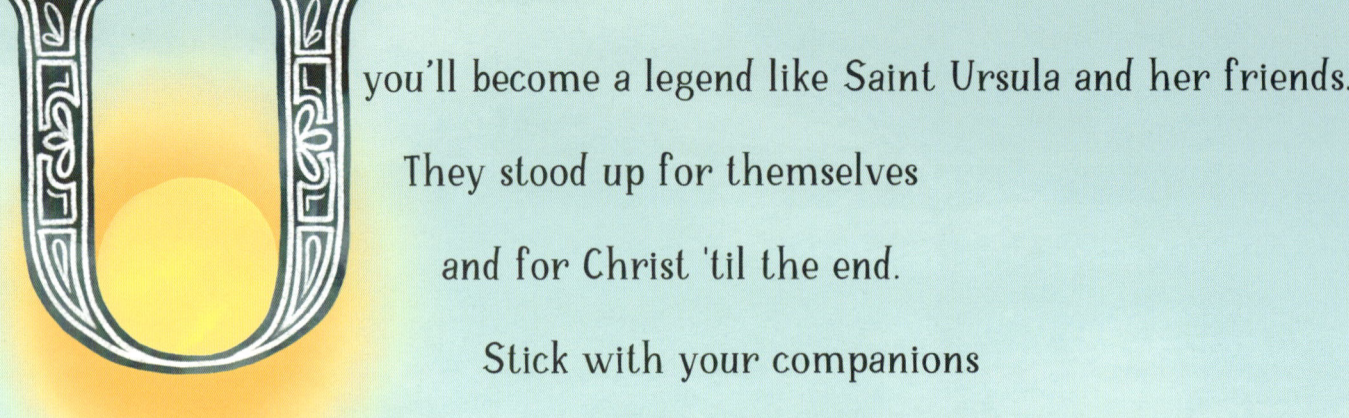

V when you're declared Venerable, you're well on your way!

With God's help you'll likely be a Blessed someday.

Known for great love and big miracles, they'll say

because you were born to be a Saint!

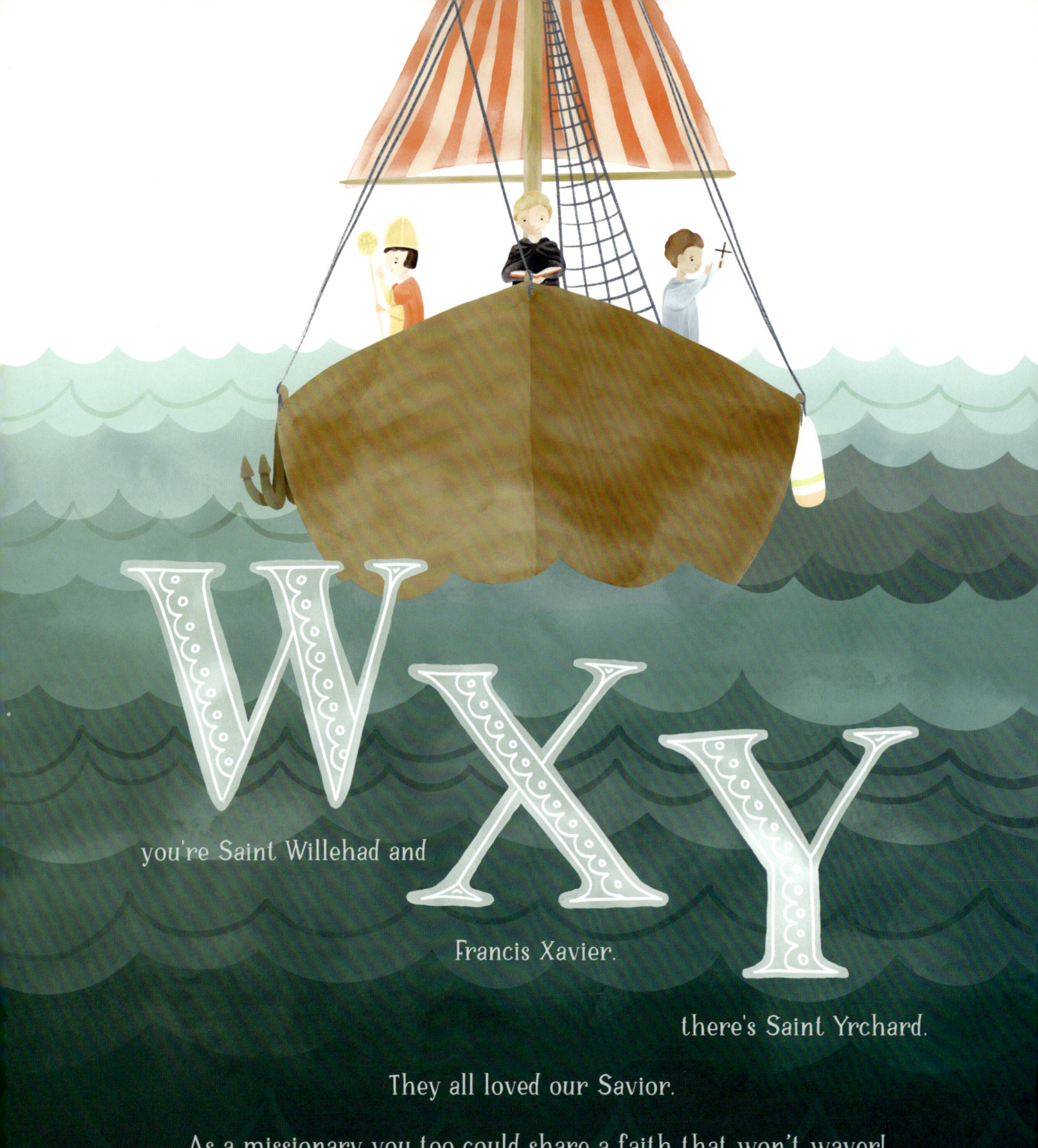

W X Y

you're Saint Willehad and Francis Xavier.

there's Saint Yrchard.

They all loved our Savior.

As a missionary you too could share a faith that won't waver!

Saints Zita and Zélie make Z come alive!

As a housekeeper and lace maker, towards God's will they both strived.

Whatever your job, God can make your work thrive

because you were born to be a Saint!

There are thousands and thousands of Saints you could be

but there is only one Saint that I think you should be.

Courageous and confident, daring and bold,

the Lord didn't make you to fill a set mold.

No, with your own unique talents and interests abounding,

He's going to use you to do something astounding.

With His Will guiding you and His Love in your heart

the best Saint you can be has been you from the start!

Featured Saints

Thomas Aquinas (1226-1274) was a quiet student drawn to philosophy and theology. While his classmates thought his quiet demeanor made him dumb, his teacher, Saint Albert the Great, knew that he would one day make big waves with his thoughts and words. Thomas went on to start his own university and write dozens of books on philosophy, theology, war, friendship, and happiness, many of which are still discussed today. This led to him becoming a Doctor of the Church. His feast day is January 28th and he is the patron of students and universities.

Adelaide of Burgundy (931-999) was married to the German King Otto and they were crowned emperors of Rome. After King Otto's death, Adelaide returned to act as regent Queen to her step-grandson and used her position to evangelize and help the poor. She also built and restored many churches. Saint Adelaide's feast day is December 16th. She is the patron of many things including princesses, prisoners, parents of large families, and step-parents.

Albert the Great (~1200 -1280) was a well-educated man from Germany. As a young adult, Albert had an encounter with the Blessed Mother that deeply moved him. After this experience he decided to become a Dominican. He went on to become a master of theology and a professor. Albert helped start multiple universities. During his life, Albert wrote many books on topics including physics, geography, astronomy, mineralogy, chemistry, biology, mathematics, scripture, philosophy, and theology. He is a Doctor of the Church and is the patron of scientists. His feast day is November 15th.

Blaise (died 316) was a doctor who became the bishop of Sebaste, Turkey. The Roman governor at the time ordered all Christians to be fed to wild beasts. Blaise fled to a cave just outside the city. There, animals flocked to him for healing of all kinds. One day Roman hunters found his cave. While the hunters were bringing Blaise to jail a woman ran to him with her son. He was choking on a fish bone. Blaise prayed, and the child was healed. While in jail, the same woman brought him a pair of candles to dispel the darkness of his cell. For his refusal to renounce his faith, Blaise was eventually beheaded. Saint Blaise is often depicted holding two crossed candles in his hands. His feast day is February 3rd. He is the patron of throat illnesses and animals.

Bernadette (1844-1879), at age 14, was gathering firewood in Lourdes, France. A bright, dazzling light shone in a small grotto full of roses near Bernadette. In the grotto appeared Mary, the Immaculate Conception. Bernadette didn't know what to do so she began praying the rosary and then Mary joined her! Bernadette returned to the grotto and continued to see Mary even when others could not. Mary told Bernadette to drink the healing waters of the spring near the grotto and to build a chapel on that spot. Millions of people now go to the grotto, spring and chapel to receive Our Lady's intercession and healing. Saint Bernadette is the patron of illness, people ridiculed for faith, and Lourdes. Her feast day is April 16th.

Thérèse of Lisieux (1873-1897) was the youngest of seven children. At the age of 14 Thérèse wanted to become a nun just like her older sisters. Being a nun didn't come easy for Thérèse. She had a hard time praying and doing big, saintly acts, so she decided she would do small acts of love. For example, not complaining, doing the tasks no one else wanted and talking to the nuns she didn't particularly like. Each of these small gestures brought her closer to Jesus! During her short life, Thérèse wrote all about her new ideas and her sister published them. Her book has changed the lives of countless people, bringing them closer to Jesus as well. The feast of Saint Thérèse is October 1st. She is the patron of florists, gardeners, and sickness.

Teresa of Ávila (1515-1582) was born into a world full of change. The western hemisphere had just begun to be explored and the protestants had broken away from the Catholic Church. Eventually, Teresa joined the Carmelite nuns and became very ill. On the brink of death, Teresa recovered and devoted herself to a life a prayer and teaching others to pray. While she was praying she often saw God and the angels! During this tumultuous time, she became like a compass for the people, always pointing them back to God. Her feast day is October 15th and she is the patron of the sick, orphans, and Spain.

Teresa Benedicta of the Cross/Edith Stein (1891-1942) was born into a Jewish family. Although Edith stopped believing in God at a young age, she had a great interest in philosophy. As an adult, her desire for truth brought her to the writings of Saint Teresa of Ávila. Edith was baptized and joined the Carmelite order several years later, just like her spiritual mentor. During World War II, Sr. Teresa Benedicta was arrested for being a Jewish convert and taken to a concentration camp. It was there that she died as a martyr, offering herself for the people of Israel. She is the patron of converted Jews, martyrs, and World Youth Day. Her feast day is August 9th.

Damien of Moloka'i (1840-1889) was born in Belgium but is best known for his work in Hawaii, where he was ordained a priest. Fr. Damien later discerned his call to serve the lepers on the island of Moloka'i. Many patients had nobody to care for them, but with Fr. Damien there, the sick were treated with dignity. The leper colony became his permanent home and eventually Fr. Damien contracted leprosy himself and died from the disease. He is the patron of people with leprosy and his feast day is May 10th.

Dymphna (7th century) was born in Ireland to a pagan father and a devout Christian mother. When Dymphna was 14 years old she consecrated herself to Jesus and took a vow of chastity. After her mother's death, her father had horribly misguided thoughts due to mental instability and bad advisors. Dymphna ran away and built a hospital to serve the poor and sick. Not long after, at the age of 15, her father found her and had her killed for refusing to return with him to be married. She is the patron of those with mental afflictions and her feast day is May 15th.

Elizabeth Ann Seton (1774-1821) was born in New York City to an Episcopal family. During her young adulthood, Elizabeth married and had five children. After her husband died, she entered the Catholic Church. Elizabeth founded the first community for religious women established in the United States and the first American Catholic School, laying the foundation for Catholic education in the U.S. She is the first person born in the United States to be canonized. Her feast day is January 4th and she is the patron of Catholic Schools.

Francis of Assisi (1181-1226) was born to a wealthy Italian cloth merchant. During his life, Francis went through a few dramatic changes, from a partying wild child to young soldier to the founder of a new religious order. Having left his family's riches behind, Francis and his followers lived off the generosity of others. He spent much of his days preaching the love of God to anyone who would listen, even if that was just the birds. A few years before his death, Francis received the stigmata (the real wounds of Christ) in his hands, feet, and side. Saint Francis is the patron of animals, birds, ecologists, and merchants. His feast day is October 4th.

Gregory the Great (540-604) was an official for Rome during his young adulthood but left to pursue a life dedicated to Christ. He became a Benedictine monk and founded six monasteries. Once Gregory was ordained a priest, he served the pope as a representative in Constantinople. At age 50 he was elected pope himself! During his papacy, Gregory removed unworthy priests, ransomed prisoners, and cared for the persecuted and dying. The title 'the Great' is given to Saints who have had a particularly large influence on the Church during their time. Saint Gregory is the patron of England, epilepsy, musicians, and teachers. His feast day is September 3rd.

Gertrude the Great (1256-1302) was a Benedictine nun in what is now Germany. She saw herself as the bride of Christ and had a profound connection to the Sacred Heart of Jesus. At age 25, she began having visions while deep in prayer. These visions continued for more than 30 years. She wrote many books but only a few survive today. Because of their influence she was given the title 'the Great,' making her the only female with this title. She is the patron of the West Indies but because of her love for the souls in Purgatory, she is often invoked to intercede for them. Her feast day is November 16th.

Helena (died 327) was born to a poor family but was made an empress by her son, Emperor Constantine the Great. Helena gave endlessly to the Church, prisoners, and the poor. When Saint Helena was given the task of finding the True Cross, she led a group to the Holy Land. There she found three crosses. In order to know which one was the True Cross, she took them to a woman with an incurable illness. Immediately, one of them cured her and that was deemed the True Cross. She also built over 80 churches in places that were significant to the life of Jesus and His Blessed Mother. Her feast day is August 18th and she is the patron of archeologists, difficult marriages, divorced people, and empresses.

Blessed Isidore Bakanja (1887-1909) was a young man from the Belgian Congo. He was evangelized by Belgian Trappist missionaries and had a deep love for Mary, the rosary, and the brown scapular. He worked for a racist, anti-Catholic employer, who demanded Isidore remove his scapular. When he refused, he was beaten until he was near death. Upon receiving Last Rites, Isidore said that he had already forgiven his attacker, promising to pray for his soul in heaven. His feast day is August 15th.

Josephine Bakhita (1869-1947) was kidnapped in her birthplace of southern Sudan at the age of 7. She was sold into slavery and given the name Bakhita. After being sold again several times, she found herself accompanying a young woman to Italy as a nanny. It was here that Bakhita discovered the Catholic Church and was baptized, taking the name Josephine. Because slavery was illegal in Italy, Josephine had found freedom at last! Josephine entered the Canossian Daughters of Charity, where she spent the remainder of her life freely serving others with a charismatic smile. Josephine is the patron of Sudan and her feast day is February 8th.

Kateri Tekakwitha (1656-1680), also known as Lily of the Mohawks, was born in present day New York. At age four, small pox tore through her village and took the lives of her family and left Kateri scarred and visually impaired. Kateri desired to know God and, at age 22, was baptized by a Jesuit missionary. Unfortunately, not all in the village were okay with her decision. She was bullied and threatened for her faith. Kateri left the village to live out her faith in Montreal, praying, serving others, and taking on many grueling acts of penance. She is the patron of Native American and First Nation Peoples, ecology, and the environment. Her feast day is July 14th.

Lidwina (1380-1433) was born in the Netherlands. At age 15 she was ice skating with friends when she fell. Crashing into the ice, she broke a rib and was sent to bed. Gangrene started to take over and Lidwina became paralyzed. She used her new circumstances to pray and offer up her suffering to God, having many mystical visions during her prayer. While she never did ice skate again, it was through this accident that she fell deeper in love with God and became the patron of ice skating and the chronically ill. Her feast day is April 14th.

Martin of Tours (316-397) was born to pagan parents in what is now Hungary but was raised in Italy. At 15, Martin entered the Roman army and was baptized at age 18. Martin eventually left the army after objecting to war and chose to be a soldier for Christ instead. He was then ordained an exorcist and monk, establishing a monastery in France where he fought against heresy. Later he became Bishop of Tours, France. Martin is one of the earliest Saints to not also be a martyr. He is the patron of soldiers and horses and his feast day is November 11th.

Nicholas Owen (died 1606) was an Englishman during a time when Catholics were persecuted in England. Wanting to do all that he could to help the Church, Nicholas used his skills to construct secret hiding places for priests, called priest holes, throughout the country. Nicholas was so good at finding the perfect places to hide, that priests often went undetected during raids. After many close calls, Nicholas was finally caught and killed for his heroic efforts. Because of his unique skills he is the patron of illusionists and escapologists. His feast day is March 22nd.

Our Lady, mother of Jesus, has revealed herself through apparitions to numerous people over the last 2,000 years! Each time, her appearance has brought about the conversion of souls and a turning back to Jesus. For an apparition to be approved by the Catholic Church there has to be a great amount of factual content found through investigation and be in accordance with Church doctrine and authority. Dozens of Marian apparitions have been recognized by the Vatican or local bishops. Eight of which are featured on Our Lady's page (Our Lady of Guadalupe, Our Lady of Fatima, Our Lady of Kibeho, Our Lady of La Salette, Our Lady of Częstochowa, Our Lady of Pontmain, Our Lady of Aparecida, and Our Lady of China).

John Vianney (1786-1859) was a priest in Ars, France. He helped lukewarm Christians take their faith more seriously after the French Revolution (a time when a lot of Catholics drifted from the Church). He is most well-known for his work as a confessor. It has been said that he would spend up to 16 hours a day in the confessional. He was truly dedicated to his work as a parish priest, which is why he is the patron of priests. His feast day is August 4th.

Padre Pio of Pietrelcina (1887-1968) was an Italian Capuchin Franciscan who was blessed with the stigmata, the real wounds of Christ, in his hands, feet, and side. People came from far and wide to see Padre Pio after the stigmata appeared. Spending up to 10 hours a day in the confessional, Padre Pio was said to have known things about the lives of the penitents that they had never mention. Other miraculous things have been attributed to Padre Pio, such as the gift of seeing Guardian Angels, levitating during deep prayer, and bilocation (the ability to be in two places at once)! His feast day is September 23rd and he is the patron of adolescents and stress relief.

John Bosco (1815-1888) was a priest in the city of Turin, where he worked tirelessly for the children of the poor. Using stage magic, John would draw in a crowd and once he had their attention, start preaching the gospel. This made him popular with the youth, and he eventually opened the Oratory of St. Francis de Sales for boys. They provided vocation education and worked to find the boys jobs and lodging. He founded the Salesians and then the Salesian Sisters to assist girls. Saint John Bosco is the patron of editors and publishers, schoolchildren, magicians, and juvenile delinquents. His feast day is January 31st.

Quirinus (died 117), for whom little is actually known, was said to be a Roman tribune ordered with executing Saints Alexander, Eventius, and Theodolus. After seeing them perform miracles in the name of God, Quirinus was baptized along with his daughter, Balbina. In time, he was beheaded for his faith and buried in the catacomb of Prætextatus. His feast day is March 30th.

Reparata (3rd century) was a virgin martyr in Palestine. Although much of what is known about her is legend, it is said that she was saved by God from being burned alive by a miraculous rain. Jailers then tried to force her to drink boiling tar but she refused. They eventually beheaded her. Her relics can be found in Nice, France and she has a sizeable devotional following in Florence, Italy making her the patron of those two cities. Her feast day is October 8th.

Sebastian (died 288) was a member of the Roman army, where he used his position to help Christians who were being persecuted by the Romans. He was a good soldier and became part of the Guard protecting the emperor. Sebastian converted many people, even other members of the Roman army. This made the emperor furious! He ordered Sebastian to be used as target practice for the archers. After his body was full of arrows, they assumed he was dead but he miraculously survived. He went back to the emperor to criticize him for persecuting Christians and was sentenced to death again. His body was later retrieved and given a proper burial. Sebastian is the patron of archers, athletes, soldiers, and police officers. His feast day is January 20th.

Teresa of Calcutta (1910-1997) was born in Albania but at age 18 joined the Loreto Sisters in Ireland. The sisters sent her to India to teach but it was the suffering that had her heart. One day Teresa heard the call of God asking her to help the poorest of the poor. Throughout the streets of India, Teresa began to care for the sick and dying, showing them love and respect. The work was hard but eventually others joined her, forming the Missionaries of Charity. For over 40 years, Mother Teresa cared for orphans and the abandoned, the diseased and the destitute. She was awarded the Nobel Peace Prize in 1979. Her feast day is September 5th and she is the patron of the Missionaries of Charity.

Ursula (died 383) is a Saint clouded in mystery. Many legends surround Ursula and the maidens that accompanied her but almost all of them agree that Saint Ursula, daughter of a Christian king, was being forced to marry a pagan prince. Ursula refused and left on a journey with many, possibly thousands, of maidens and ladies in waiting. On this journey, pagan Huns tried to force her to marry their chieftain. She and her companions were killed for her refusal. Her feast day is October 21st and she is the patron of archery, British Virgin Islands, and Cologne, Germany.

Venerable Antonietta Meo (1930-1937) was born into a religious Italian family. Due to cancer, Antonietta had to have her left leg amputated at age six. Already, she knew that suffering was a powerful tool when offered to Jesus. She began elementary school with an uncomfortable prosthetic leg. In quick succession that year, Antonietta received her First Holy Communion and Confirmation. The tumor from her cancer continued to spread throughout her body and she died before the age of seven.

Venerable Augustus Tolton (1854-1897) was born into a family of slaves in Missouri. Escaping from his life of slavery, he went on to study for the priesthood in Rome (having been turned away from all U.S. seminaries). Augustus was ordained at Saint John Lateran Basilica at 31 years old and celebrated his first mass at Saint Peter's Basilica. He returned to the United States to serve in Chicago and is recognized as the first known Black priest in America!

Venerable Edel Quinn (1907-1944) was born in Ireland to a Catholic family. At a time in her young adulthood when her faith was becoming stagnant, she joined the Legion of Mary, a lay apostolic group. Although she had developed tuberculosis, Edel answered the call to go as a missionary to Africa. Starting in Kenya and working her way through Uganda, Tanzania, Malawi, and Mauritius, Edel established hundreds of Legion branches before losing her seven year battle with tuberculosis.

Willehad of Bremen (735-789) was a Benedictine bishop and missionary. Although he was from England, Willehad journeyed as a missionary to both the Frisians of the Netherlands and the Saxons of Germany. Because of violent uprisings in both instances, he was forced to flee. Willehad went on to be the bishop of Worms, Germany. He is the patron for the German state of Saxony and his feast day is November 8th.

Francis Xavier (1506-1552) was a good friend of Saint Ignatius of Loyola, who was the man responsible for Francis's conversion to Christianity. He joined Ignatius's community, the Society of Jesus and became a priest. Francis spent the next 10 years as a missionary bringing the faith to people in Portugal, India, Malaysia and Japan. He served the sick and poor with joy. He is one of the patrons of missionaries as well as Japan, jewelers, and sailors. His feast day is December 3rd.

Yrchard (5th century), also known as Saint Erthard or Irchard, was born to pagan parents in Scotland but found Christianity in his youth. Becoming a priest and then bishop, Yrchard, went on to serve as a missionary among the Picts, an ancient Scottish people. His feast day is August 24th.

Zélie Guerin Martin (1831-1877) was a mother of nine and wife to Saint Louis Martin. During their marriage they lost four children. These tragedies strengthened their marriage and knit their family closer together. All five of her surviving daughters entered the convent and her youngest daughter would grow up to be Saint Thérèse! Zélie was a talented lace maker and started her own very successful business. She and Saint Louis are the patrons of married couples and share of feast day of July 12th.

Zita (died 1278) was born to a poor, Christian family. At the age of twelve Zita began work as a servant, taking on the role of housekeeper. She was known as a patient, pious, and generous worker. Even with her work schedule Zita managed to attend Mass daily and pray throughout her duties. She also gave generously to the poor and helped the sick and imprisoned. Zita is the patron of domestic workers, maids, and servants. Her feast day is April 27th.

Process to Canonization

First, the person's local bishop investigates and finds them to be worthy of being a Saint.

Second, the Congregation for the Causes of Saints can choose to begin their own investigation of the person's life. At this point the person may be called **Servant of God**.

Third, if the Congregation for the Causes of Saints approves of the candidate, they can declare that the person lived a virtuous life and that they pursued holiness while here on earth. The person may be called **Venerable**.

Fourth, a miracle must be proven to have taken place through the intercession of that person. The miracle is usually a healing by nature. The healing has to be scientifically unexplainable while also being instantaneous and permanent. Independent doctors, theologians and ultimately the pope, must approve this miracle before they can be declared a **Blessed**.

Fifth, a second miracle is needed in order to declare someone a **Saint**. The confirmation of a second miracle goes through the same scrutiny as the first.